What's That Sound?

by Joanna Lake

illustrated by Genie Espinosa

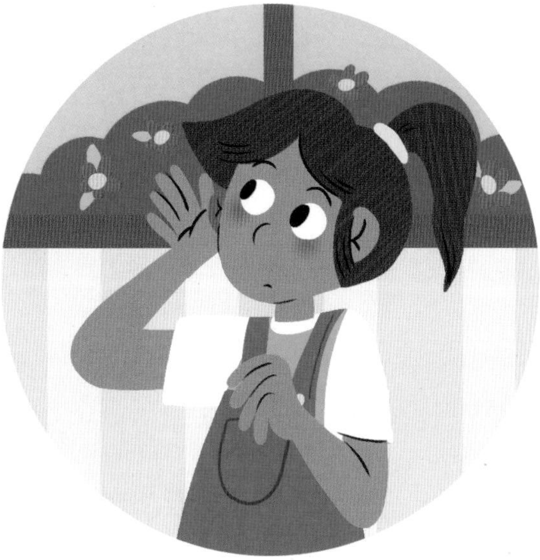

OXFORD
UNIVERSITY PRESS
AUSTRALIA & NEW ZEALAND

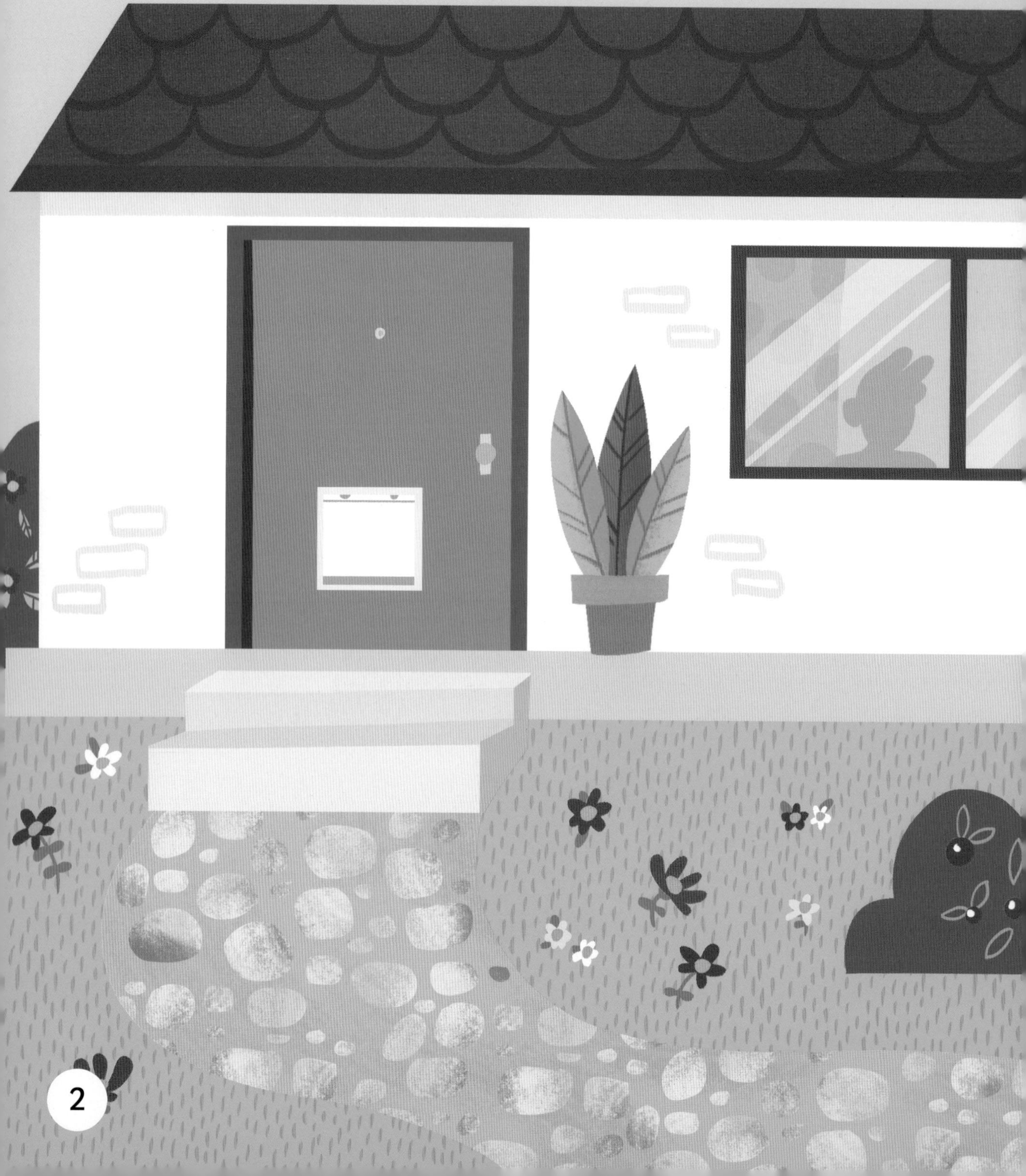

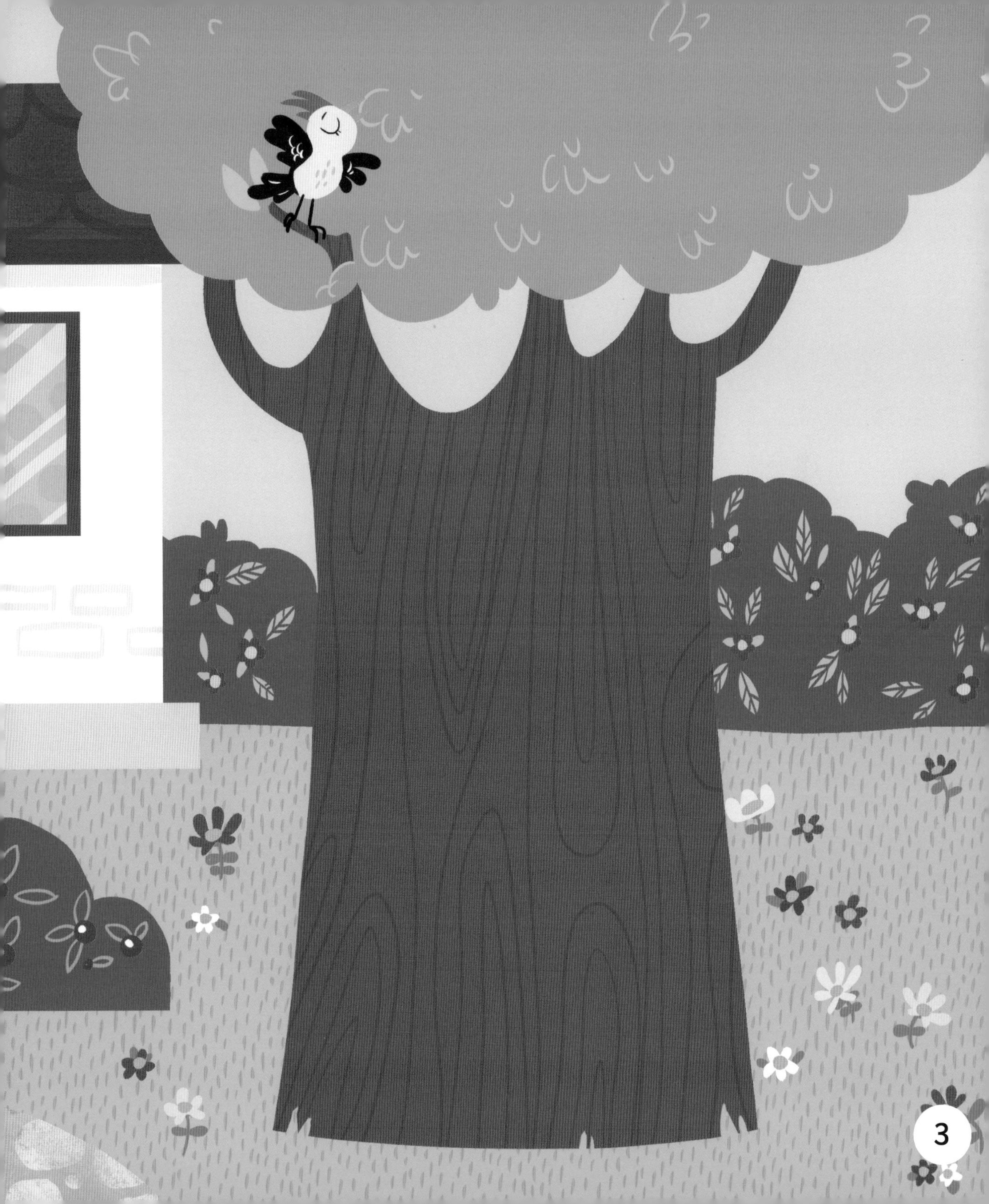

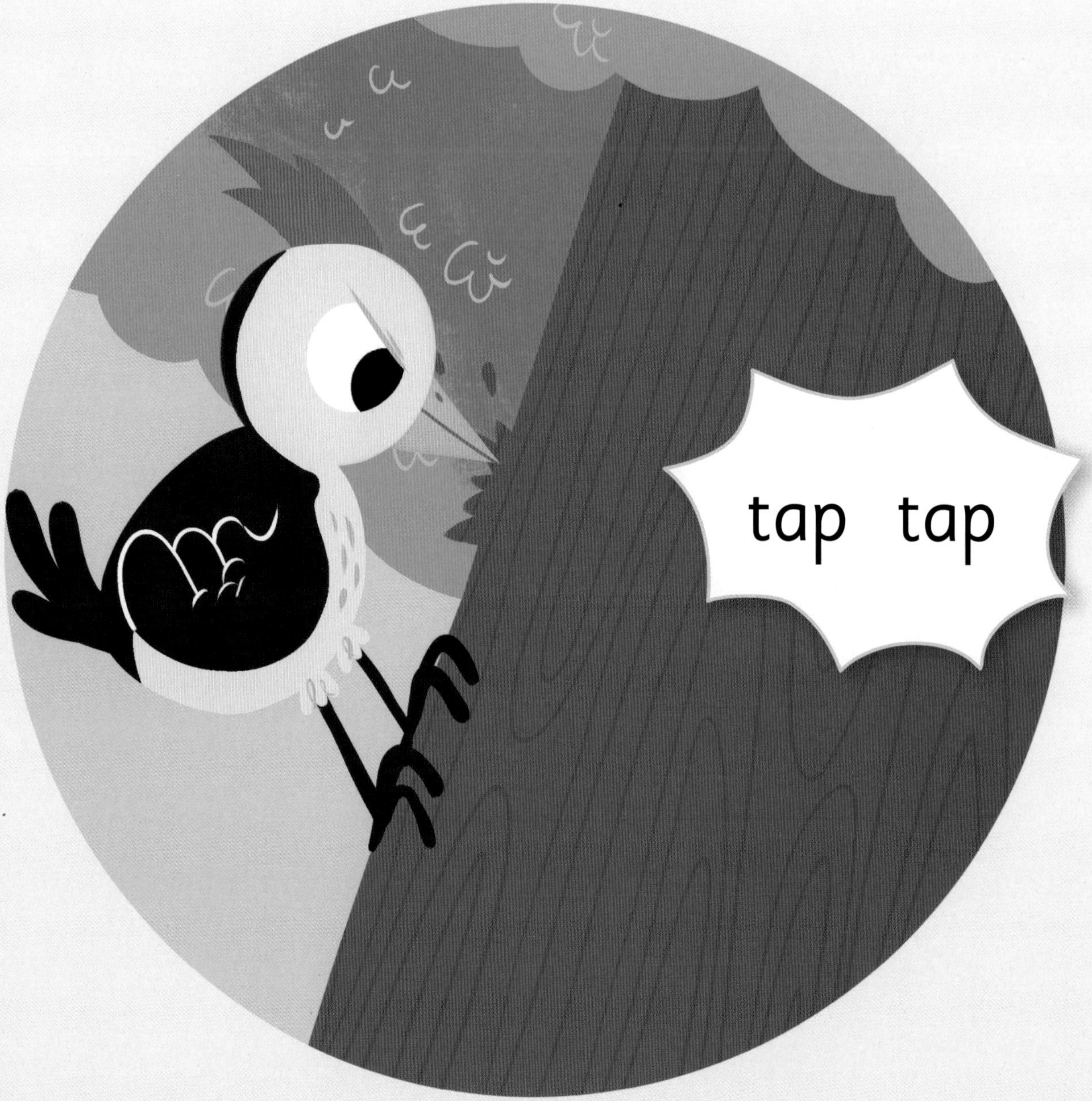
tap tap

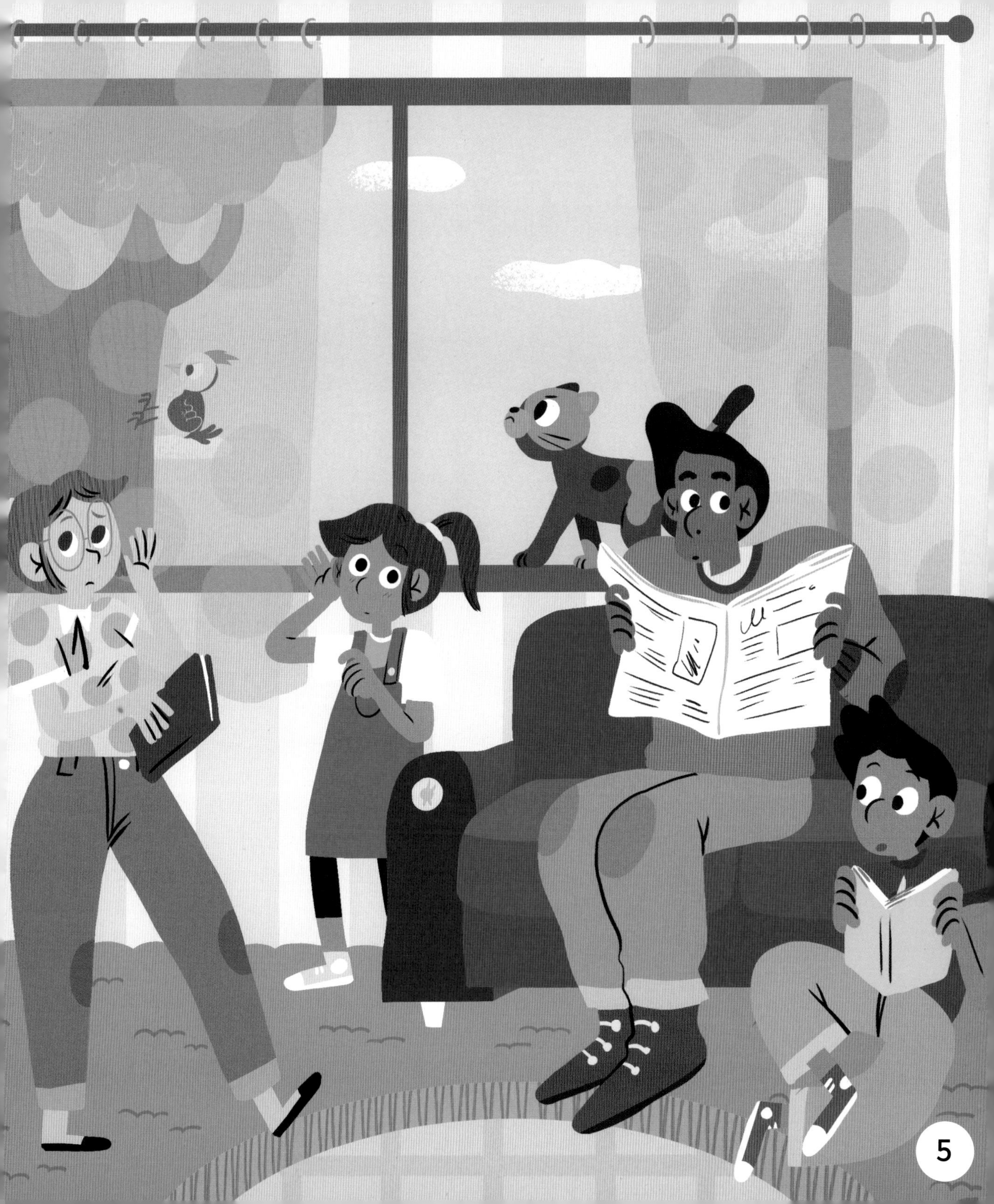

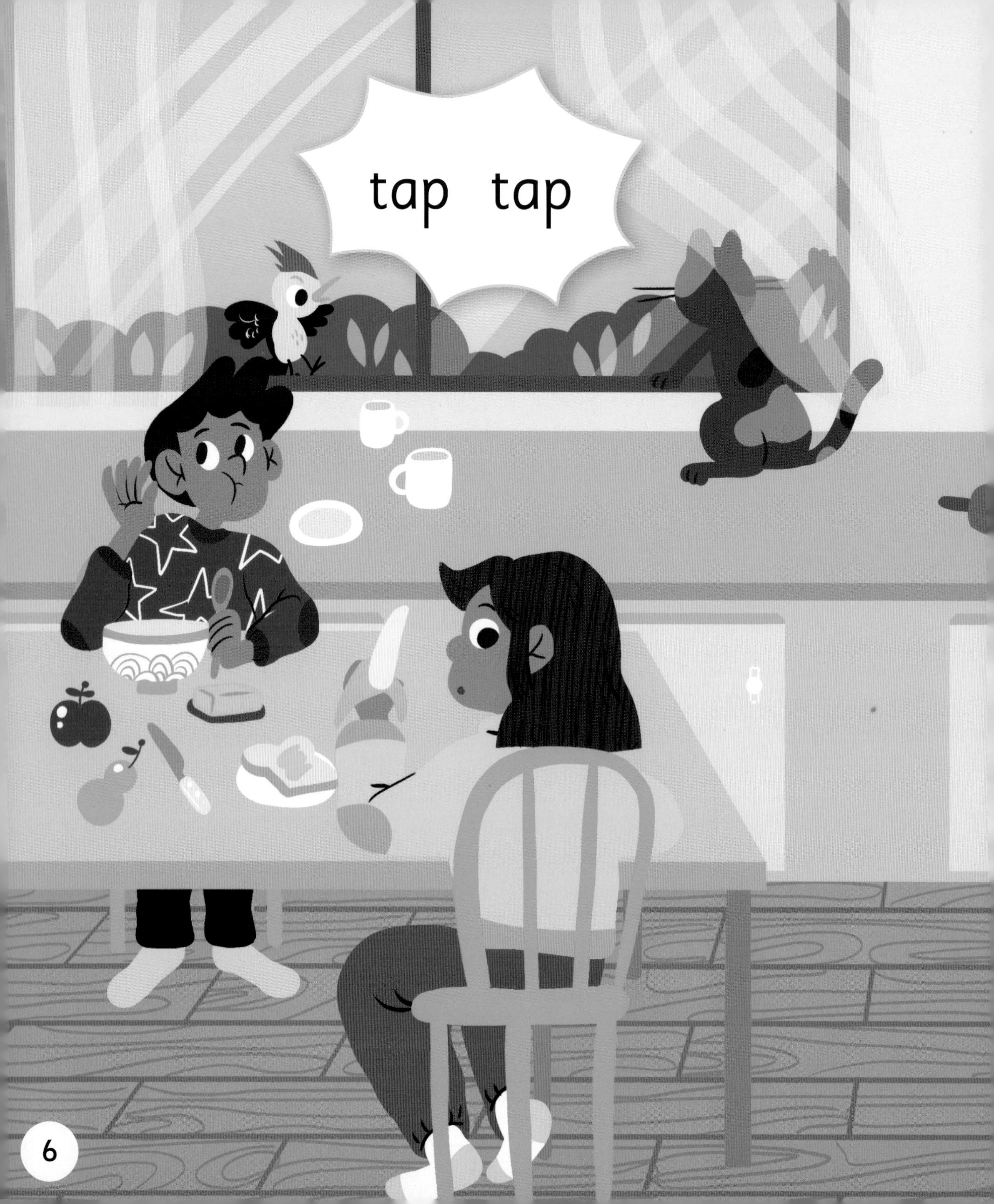
tap tap

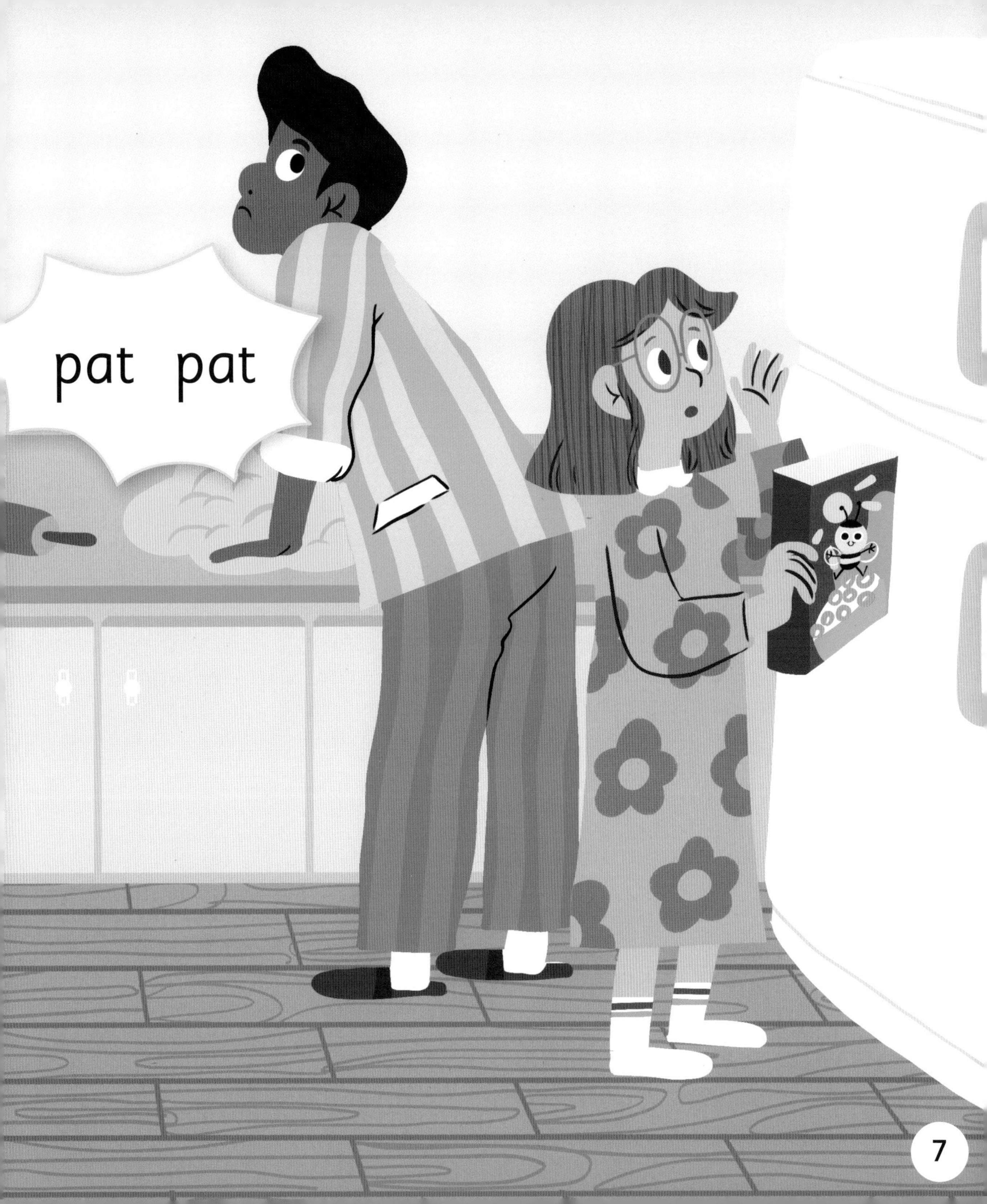
pat pat

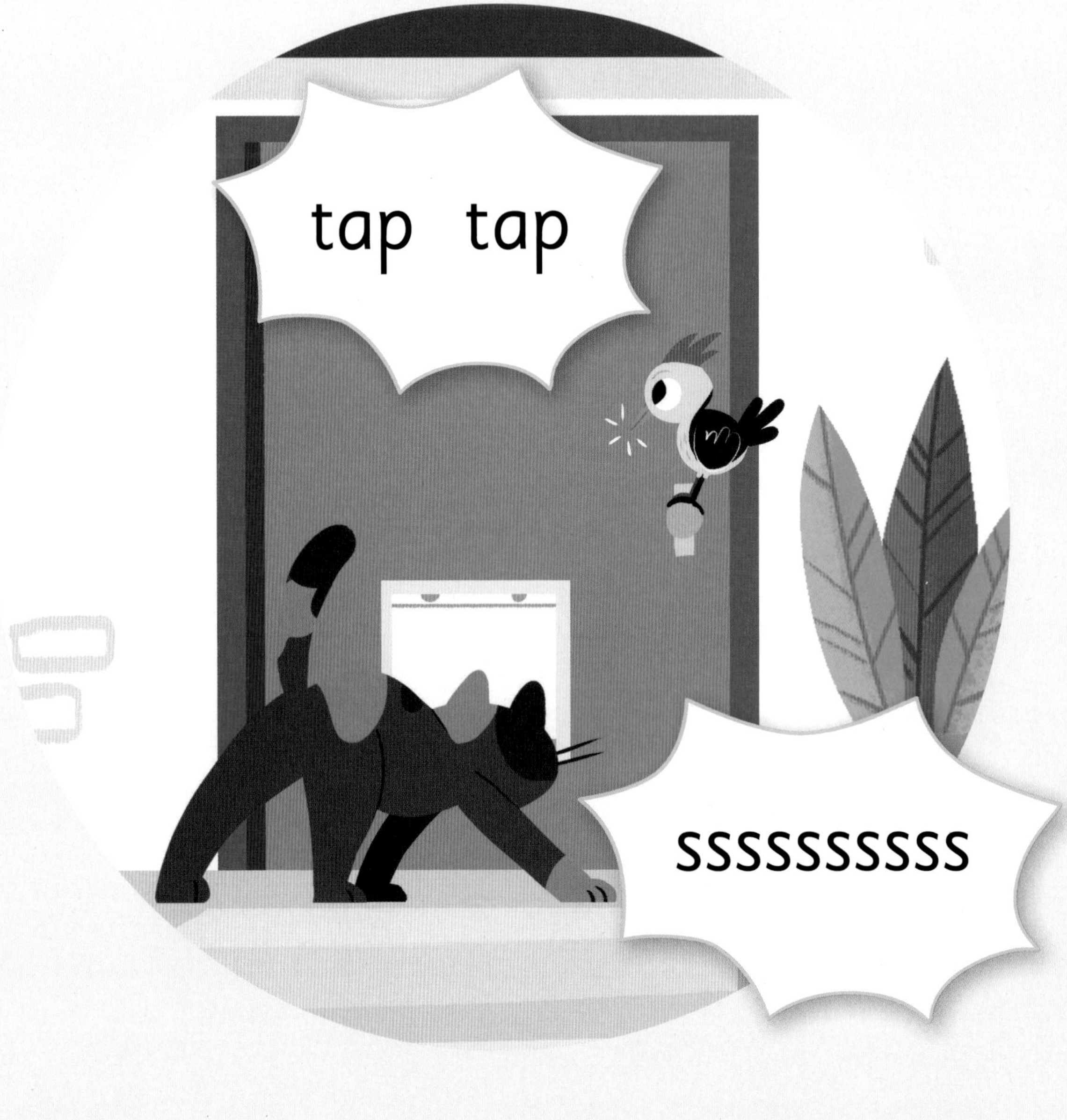
tap tap
sssssssss

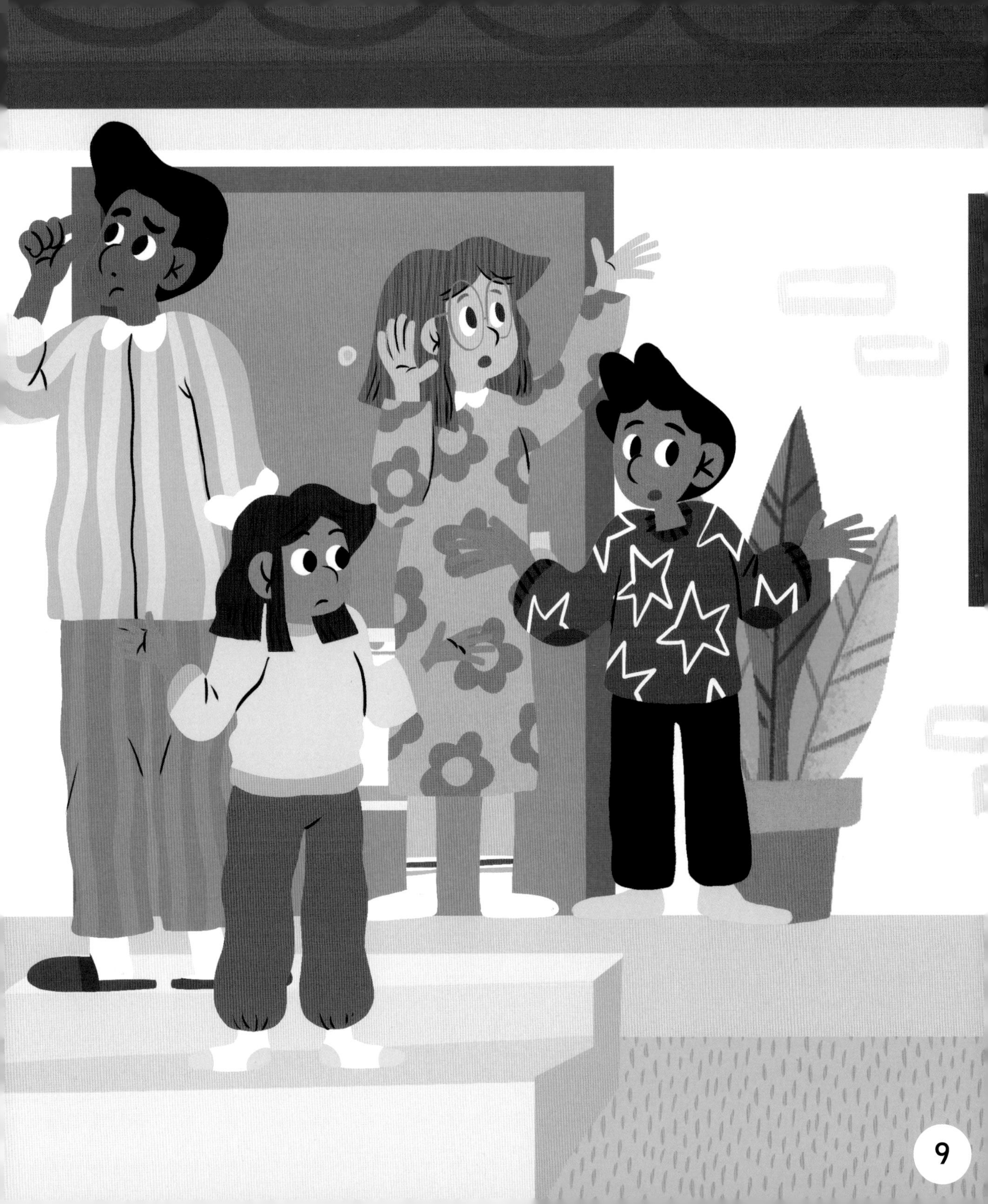

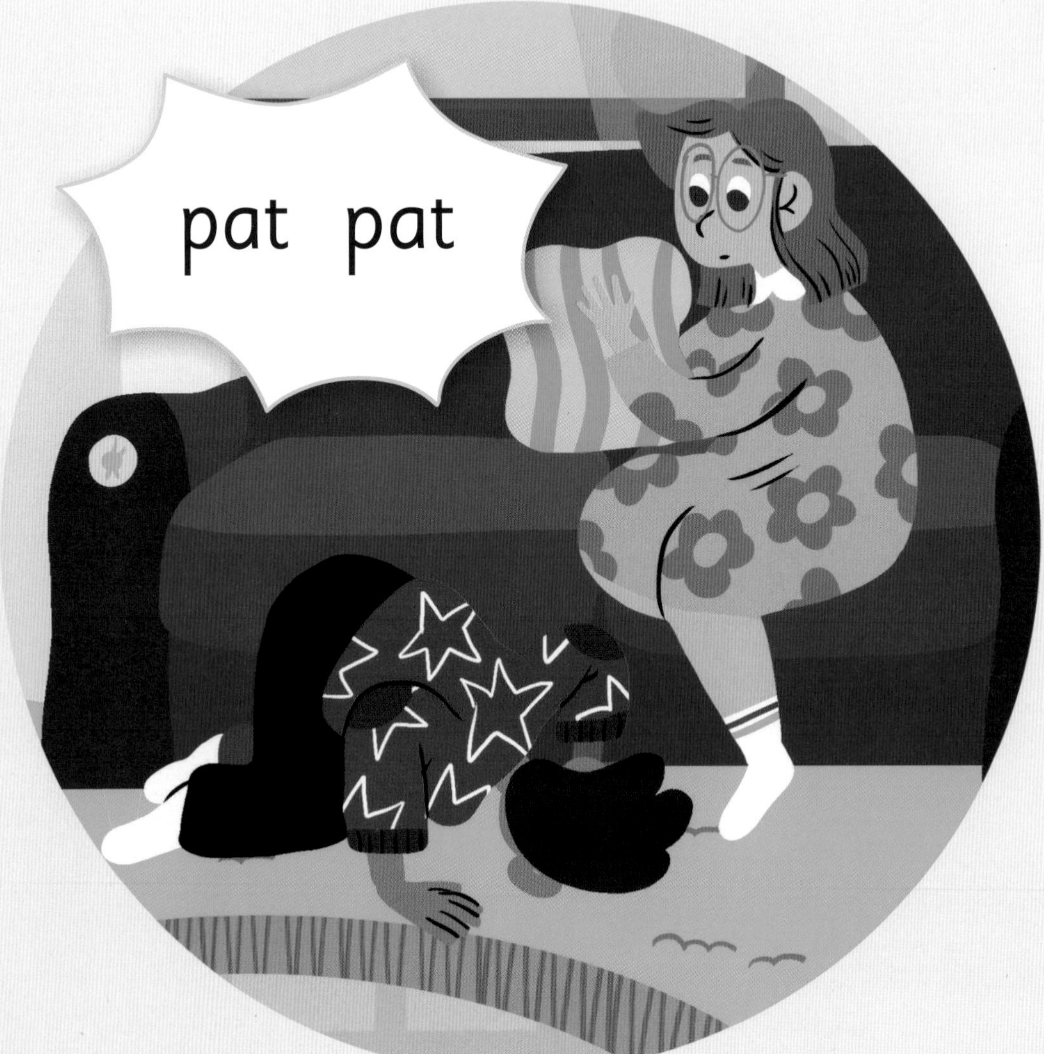
pat pat

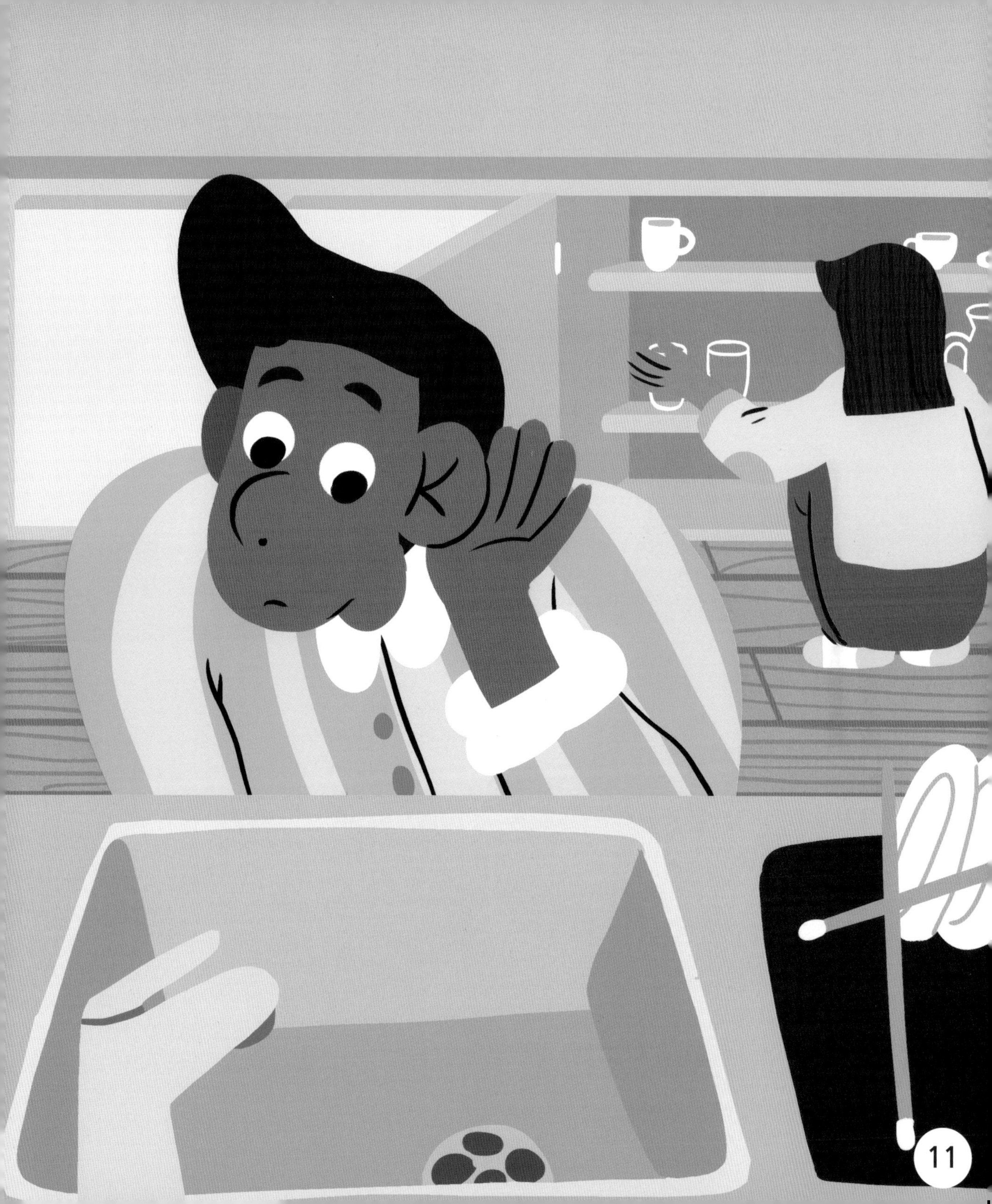

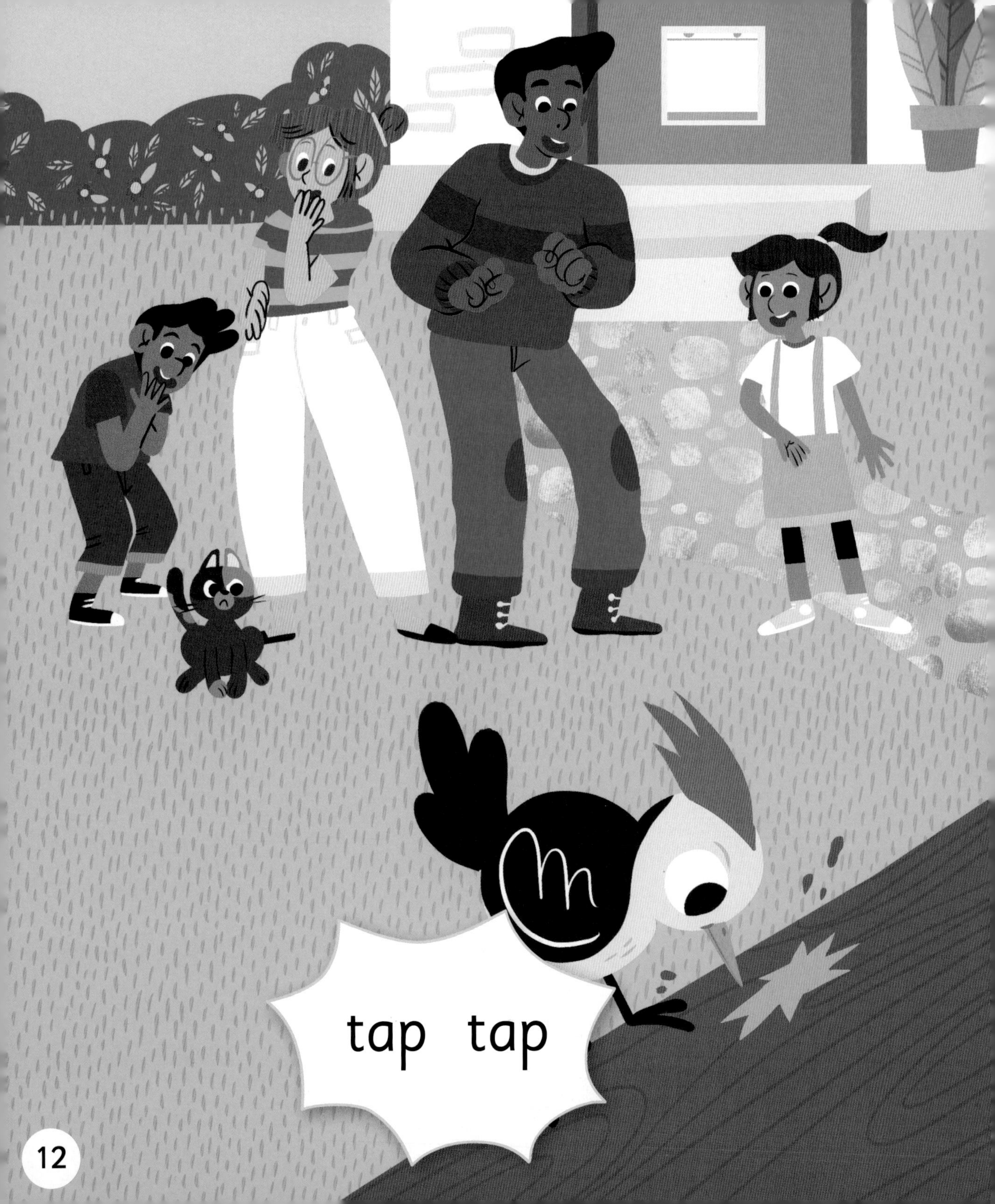
tap tap